Living In the Lyte
Lessons in Life, Love and Truth

By Lana "MC Lyte" Moorer

Publisher:	Sunni Gyrl, Inc.
Publisher Address:	14431 Ventura Blvd #120
Publisher City, State, Zip:	Sherman Oaks, CA 91423
Website:	www.mclytenow.com
Phone:	855.MCLYTE1
ISBN 13:	978-0-9773232-4-1

Editor:	**Lynn Richardson**

*This book is dedicated to Sunni and to all of my fans across the world who have shown me love continuously throughout the years. In this book, I have shared some of my inner most thoughts and hopefully you will **"live in your light"** on your way to achieve all that God has in store for you.*

MC LYTE

Inside This Lyte

WELCOME

You are only as beautiful as your thoughts.

As I began to write this book, I wondered about the concept of being completely truthful and transparent. I wondered what it would mean to lay it all on the line and not care about the repercussions. I just wanted to take off whatever may have blocked the truth from being told and the honesty from shining through.

Living in the Light . . . what does that mean? It's an awakening with everything set forth for all to see. It means being okay with the absolutes in your life and being willing to share and talk about the wins and the losses.

Personally, *Living in the LYTE* means I am totally free to be ME. Today, I live my life for all to see in hopes that others will learn that even when I fall, God always gives me the strength to rise again. It wasn't always like this. There were times when I hid, when I lived in the dark, and when I hid moments that should have been celebrated.

Living in the Lyte / Light is simply translated as living in truth: where truth prevails and every decision is based on "what is" and not "what if." There were times when I made choices that I was not proud of and I felt as though it wouldn't benefit anyone to know about those times. How wrong I was to think there would be nothing for another person to learn by way of my mistakes and mishaps.

I can honestly say that in this stage of life, I am well aware when I have deviated from the path -- the path that is intended for me: a path that only I can walk and a path that is prepared, designed and ordained for me to learn, live and grow through. I've accomplished plenty throughout this blessed life of mine, but I can admit that when problems do exist, they exist around relationships. Relationships with business, intimacy, family and friendship. As long as there have been 2 people on this earth, there has been the need for relationships. Relating to others can be quite an ordeal, but what I've learned through it all is that every relationship is different yet necessary for the growth of everyone involved.

With business, the need to relate to everyone in my company is major. From top to bottom, I've got to perfect how to communicate and listen to all of the voices swarming around me. In order to stay in tune with it all, I have to be present and in that lies the need to deal with the truth. I've come to know that the light is all around me if I'm willing to see it.

Another reason I choose to live this God given life in the light is so I can learn, just like others, what it means to be loved for who I truly am. The realization that I cannot truly be loved if no one truly knows who I am has aided in my awareness. Part of learning to love all of me means I need to completely be myself. If that means I am goofy and silly, so be it. If it means I enjoy being quiet and I don't always find the need to talk, so be it. The key is this: whatever I am, I am going to be all of it and not try to present myself in a cool and cute package, but rather in a state that is real and consistent.

Living in the Lyte takes an in depth look at why it's so important to live a life that you can be proud of: a life that is open, free and without restraints. It reinforces that the rules you set should be set by you and for you, and not by others who seek to put you in a box or to dictate your parameters. You, yourself, can create the rules -- mediated by love, truth and light -- that will help you throughout this beautiful journey of life.

With the exception of some vegetables, all good things grow in the light. Plant life, new thoughts, new concepts and new depths of freedom all grow in the light. I cannot think of one living organism that can continue to grow in darkness. Without light, all is sure to wither away.

Between the covers of this book, I will share some of the most personal epiphanies that helped me to come closer to living a fuller and more truthful life. This book is, undoubtedly, the most candid word ever written by me to be seen by another. My hope is that you will be able to learn from my experiences and make choices that shape a life in the light.

TRUTH IN LYTE

*Whatever you do in the dark will
eventually come into the light.*

There's a great purpose for each of us.
To walk in that purpose means we will
have to take the walk in the light. For
some, it will mean walking through dark
hallways and dimly lit tunnels to get to
that light, but what we can count on is
that there is light at the end of it all; we
just have to be willing to put the work in.

Facing your own demons can make for a
disturbing factor when you finally see the
YOU in it all. For example, you may
realize that everything you've ever
thought or said that was ill-intended
towards another living being was actually
your frustration with yourself. You may
have spoken ill of others because of the

lack and unhappiness that existed in your own world. When you finally admit to being your own problem after all the years of blaming other people is when you can finally come alive. You then begin to own YOU again - your thoughts, your decisions, your actions, and your intentions -- and refocus your path in the direction of purposeful light.

Long ago I had asked God for an anointing, which He delivered. As time went on and I became more recognizable, however, I began to wish for something different: I wanted to walk the streets of New York City without being stopped every 5 feet!! I secretly wished I were no longer recognizable and before long my wish had been granted. The truth is there are no secrets. Whatever one thinks becomes real. What you believe and what's in your heart is what will eventually show up -- in the light.

Who was I to not want the recognition and privileges that resulted from the talent God had so lovingly bestowed upon me?!? I had the power to influence the hip hop community for generations and beyond. How could I ignore the reality that He had brought it all to fruition? How ungrateful I had become, due to stardom being a heavy cross to bear. I had quickly forgotten about the long nights in the studio recording the hits throughout the early part of my career. I had forgotten about licking stamps to send records and responding to hundreds of fans who had sent letters from near and far.

I had simply forgotten about the arduous work that had taken place by everyone who was involved. The sleepless nights and long days spent promoting, marketing and branding the latest hit that would be another MC Lyte sensation. The team had worked long and hard to create this buzz and I had chosen to push it away without considering all the sacrifices that had been made by others.

A moment of reality struck me as I stood at that crossroad in my life and career. That moment is when I chose to live in the light, which meant I needed to find the exact truth about the entire ordeal, about how I was feeling, and about why I was feeling that way. Living in the light meant accepting the truth of knowing that I had been an absolute brat. I should have been grateful and when things became stressful, I should have searched for ways to be better and to celebrate all that had been done for me. I should have been thankful to have accomplished so much at such a young age. When I realized this, I quickly embraced all that had been done for me because the truth was I had an amazing career that was built by a group of people who believed in me and wanted the best for me. They stopped at nothing to bring home the gold and had chosen to put their time, energy and effort into me.

The reality was I had acquired fans who loved my music because it had influenced them and somehow made their life experiences better. I had participated in altering their state of mind and bringing a sense of happiness, enjoyment, or contentment.

That was the first truth I faced about my career; the second was coming into an enormous amount of integrity. After requesting to be released from my record label of 13 years, my request had been granted. It was highly unusual, I might add, to gain a release from a label during the mid-stream promotion of a new project. Unbeknownst to anyone, I had a promissory deal waiting in the wings with Will Smith. Will and I had been friends since the late 80s when we toured the nation with MC Hammer, Heavy D and many others. Will had a new label and he told me that if I ever became unhappy with or ready to split from my existing label, I'd always have a home with his.

After a year of negotiation and a year of recording, before long, with lots of hard work, we had an album. I had traveled to Virginia to work with Teddy Riley and the Neptunes. I went to Philly to work with Jazzy Jeff's camp and while there I met, then unsigned, Jill Scott. I traveled to Atlanta and worked with the brightest and most innovative talent on the come up.

All for not! Right around the time the album was near completion, Will's label parted ways with its distributor. For me, it was horrific and the timing was awful. At that time, the state of California mandated that record labels were required to give musicians signed to their labels a monthly stipend, and my stipend was just shy of $15,000 monthly. I began to harbor feelings of leaving. Distribution had gone sour for the label and there were no signs of recovering that major missing part. No label could exist without a distribution channel to release records and meet the demand of the consumers. Time was slipping by very quickly and I felt I needed to move fast before my entire career started flashing before me. My last release was in 1998 and it was now 2001. So much time had been spent preparing for this new project, yet there weren't any distribution channels set up for release.

The most important thing I learned throughout this situation was this: you've got to clear the slate of what's old and not working if you desire anything new and lasting to feed your true purpose. I wanted to actively get out there and shop my record for a new deal, however I knew I needed to bring closure to the deal I was in with Overbrook Records, owned by Will Smith. Terminating the deal with Overbrook meant I would no longer receive the monthly stipend which I needed to survive. It meant I would potentially leave a bitter taste in the label's mouth because I wasn't exemplifying patience. I felt my time escaping and I felt like I needed to move quickly.

I decided to call the label's president and let him know my intentions. It would have been disgraceful for me to get out there and start shopping my record without the label knowing. I knew better than to start that type of drama. I wanted everyone to be happy in the end -- so, the less drama, the better.   So I called and stated I wanted out. I stressed that I needed to find a home for my record. I asked for two graces in particular: 1) to own the songs we had spent a year recording; and 2) that I be given one more stipend check and then I'd be on my way.

It was the ethical thing to do. Many suggested that I should have said nothing, shopped my record, and continued to receive the monthly check so I could guarantee that my basic expenses would be taken care of until I found another deal. But something about accepting money and knowing I had intentions of finding a deal elsewhere didn't sit right in my spirit. I needed to release them from the obligation of delivering something they couldn't deliver. Aside from that, the deal wasn't about getting paid. For me, the deal was about releasing new music and getting out there to perform for my fans. It was about someone finally hearing this extraordinary body of work that had been recorded. Thank God . . . they granted my release, gave me ownership of the music and sent me one more check. That was living in the light: being led by the truth that resided in my spirit and not compromising or going with what appeared to be the easy route.

What an extremely rewarding experience it was for me to live in the light and behave admirably as I continued to pursue my purpose. If you find yourself in a situation that doesn't feel comfortable, a place where your spirit is not at ease, it means you should probably do a quick **"GUT CHECK."** Not necessarily in the sense of your physical gut, but your innate, spiritual gut. But that's not to say you should ignore your physical gut: if your stomach feels funny when you know you are about to do something you shouldn't, or make an unethical decision, then pay attention. Check to make sure whatever you're doing is a behavior or reaction that is in line with your spiritual agenda. If you find you're uncomfortable, ask:

1. Has something like this happened before?
2. What were the results?
3. What can I do to bring ease?
4. Would I be happy or pleased if I was on the other end of this decision?

Play chess, not checkers. Don't make quick moves. Think about how one move could impact the next five or six moves and how one move could ultimately set you up for long term failure or success. If you've gone through a similar circumstance then it's time for further investigation.

1. Why am I uncomfortable?
2. What could be the outcome if I continue to be ok with feeling uncomfortable?
3. How much time, energy and effort will be wasted if I don't fix this NOW?
4. What can I do now to bring peace to my soul and understanding to those around me?

If it's strength that you need to help you make the right decision, then how can you acquire it? Who can you talk to that you can trust to help you understand the truth in a fair and impartial manner? Most times, talking honestly about the situation can bring a better understanding about what you want and need in your life to feel whole.

There is something so sacred about advancing in life with truth. Everything about it feels so right. Every step, every breath and every move is geared towards love and honesty which all makes living more appealing. Life becomes one huge canvas for nothing but creative energy to flow with fluidity towards your purpose.

TRUE LYTE ALWAYS SHINES

BE READY . . .
So you'll never have to get ready.

There have been so many times throughout my career when I wasn't the person who was chosen for a particular opportunity. There were times when I didn't get the job and the truth is that in most of those cases, I was not ready. But in life, there will always be the crowd of folks who will let you know when something should have been given to you: an award, praise or recognition. In some ways, those people want build your confidence and make you feel good about who you are, but be careful: their "pump-ups" might cause more trouble than help. I call them EGO BOOSTERS. Do you really need "yes" people around while you are striving for excellence? Although they mean well, they do not have the understanding that if in fact "it" were yours, you'd actually have it. They are quick to say you should have gotten that role, job, or spot and damn to the other person who did receive it. The EGO BOOSTER may even tell you that the person who won really didn't deserve it, and to make matters worse, they even attempt to convince us that those who chose, chose wrong. How crazy and janky is that?!? I once read that one should seek his own counsel and this is one of those times you actually should. If you want to challenge your light to keep shining, you might want to quiet the noise that come from others who say you should have received something that you didn't after the fact.

It took a while for me to truly understand that if I did not get the job I was after, then that job wasn't meant for me and I wasn't meant for it at that particular time.

Perhaps I wasn't prepared or perhaps someone else was better qualified -- simple as that. In either case, trusting that whatever God had for me would be mine was an important milestone for me to cross. We must know that once we have prepared and then rightfully earned our position, there is absolutely nothing that can occur to make it go away.

Juxtapose; we should also be aware that even if we study, prepare and pray, the winnings still may go to another. Life is a game and a game means that inevitably, there will be competition. There isn't a profession in existence that is void of competition. Every where you are, there are people who do what you do, who match your skill set, or who may even do it better. When I say better, I mean, quicker with more efficiency. I mean they are willing to put in longer hours which shows tenacity and commitment. Doesn't matter if it's entertainment, banking, real estate or education . . . competition is in effect.

There were times when I knew for sure that I just was not ready for certain acting roles. I was either ill-prepared or didn't believe I could even have the role I was up for; therefore I sabotaged my chances before I even began. While preparing for some roles I would actually picture another actor that I'd pick if I were the casting director, how absurd is that?! I had ideas that I wasn't the 'girl next door' and that's what most Hollywood roles called for. I'd make up excuses for myself as to why I'd just go in and get it over with because clearly I did not fit the character description. I often thought it was funny that they'd call me in to read for roles I was so obviously wrong for. Had I gone in with a better attitude and a belief system of expectancy, who knows if I would have been chosen. I might have been just the person they were searching for.

With all of that baggage, I was not living in the light. At that time, I felt getting a role would have justified why I had moved to Los Angeles. It would have put the naysayers to rest who hadn't heard music from me and thought I had completely disappeared. I halfway wanted the role, yet it was for all the wrong reasons, none of which included the premise that I really enjoyed acting. Me winning the role was to somehow prove to the public that I was still worthy and that not all had been loss. I was still in the frame of mind of caring what people thought about my success when in fact NO ONE cared. I was looking for validation from others, when really, I just needed to believe in myself.

I can recall a time when I showed up more than prepared for a role on a new sitcom. I spent a week prepping for the role, meeting with an acting coach and studying lines into the late night hours. One thing about me, if I have an audition coming up, I eat, breathe and sleep that role until I've actually completed the process. I was so excited about this new role and what it would mean if I actually won the spot that I even walked around in character.

I rocked the first round of auditions and was immediately asked to stay for another round. When casting asks you to stick around, that's a great sign. It also means a few folks will be asked to leave which means they didn't get a role and they now have to leave the offices so the crew can carry on with the actors they are really interested in seeing again.

After reading for the second round, the casting director contacted my agent and asked me to return for a network read. A network read meant I had already made it past the producers and the last stop was a room full of network heads that would literally make the final decision. Technically if you make it all the way to the network, you've done a great job.

I continued to study and I made a huge attempt to check my nerves at the door when I showed up for the last of the auditions. There were lots of actors at the office and it seemed as though the casting crew called in 3 choices for each role. This is done to mix and match characters so they can find the exact pairing of actors who will work for their project. Usually height, weight, skin hue / color can all play a factor. By this time, if you've made it to the network, there isn't a question of whether or not you're a good actor. The question is, does every one aesthetically belong? Do these people look as if they've been friends or even know one another for that matter? Much like the hit series FRIENDS, I'm sure the casting company met with hundreds of actors searching for the exact chemistry that would create what would appear to be an on-camera friendship between what clearly could have been 6 strangers.

The two other women up for the same role that I was up for were actresses Tasha Smith and Tracy Ellis Ross and the show was "GirlFriends." Clearly we are all extremely different from one another -- and that was the intended goal: for casting to show the network they had found strong actors who varied in aesthetics and styles.

When it was all said and done, I knew I had done my absolute best. I studied and delivered some of my best work for that character. Though I mourned the loss of the role I couldn't get trapped in the system of thinking I was inadequate. It's very easy as an artist to get caught in believing you just weren't good enough. Some equate not getting the role or job with not being good and really, sometimes your level of expertise has absolutely nothing to do with it. The decisions that happen on the other side of the door have so much more to do with just talent and unfortunately, artists take it to heart and some find it difficult to recover. My answer to not receiving something I feel I deserve is this: Live in the Light. This merely means to live in the truth and in this case the truth was Tracey Ellis Ross was their choice, period, point blank. I don't need to make any other excuses about why I felt I was ready or fit for that role. I don't need to put myself down and wallow in how I could have done that differently and said that line another way and moved my body in that direction during that sentence . . . yada yada yada. Letting go of it all allowed me to be free. It freed me up spiritually and mentally for the next opportunity. Not too long after, I landed a role on the series "For Your Love" alongside Holly Robinson Pete. That role was written for me and there was no way to not be great.

My studying and classes paid off and I left a lasting impression with TV show creator Yvette Bowser and when she created her new sitcom Half & Half, she thought of me and offered me a substantial role. That role was made for me and there was nothing that could hinder or impede upon the execution of it.

Many years ago I auditioned for casting director Robi Reed for the role of Cleo in Set it Off. After seeing Queen Latifah perform the role, I knew without a shadow of doubt that there was no way on earth I was right or ready for that role. There have been many roles and opportunities that I wasn't ready for and those moments taught me that I needed to get ready and stay ready. I know you've heard it time in and time out: LUCK, there is no such thing. On the other hand, there have been roles I've won and roles I've turned down; thus those slots became opportunities for others who were ready and not lucky.

Luck is being ready when the opportunity knocks and nothing else defines the word. Knowing when you're ready takes looking at one's self with honest eyes. More times than not I meet people who want to be famous and believe the route to that existence is through entertainment. But not just in entertainment, they actually bank on being successful performers who work in front of the cameras. I always ask them to take a long, hard and HONEST look at what they have to contribute to the world of entertainment: can it compete with what's out there today?! Though are many entertainers but there are far fewer who are actually stars. I then ask, how can you garner fame with what it is that you're great at? To take it a step further, when you discover what it is that you do that can serve others, there lies your ability to tap into fame. Bill Gates is famous and it didn't take singing to get him there. Steve Jobs was and still remains famous for turning the world of technology over on its head. The truth will always work, so working within the confines of what's real to you is vital.

The most any of us can do is prepare ourselves and work diligently until we attain the results that we're looking for. We can listen and learn from people who have done it and who are doing it. There is always someone we can look to for tips on becoming who we aspire to be. What I'm merely saying is open yourself to the experience of learning in an arena where you may have thought learning was the last thing you'd do. It means listening when you'd rather talk. The saying I've heard and read all throughout my adult life, "Be interested, not interesting" means to let your performance rest on intermission and see what the light of truth is willing to show you. Breathe easy in the present moment and take everything in so you can make better decisions in a timely fashion. Love your surroundings and whatever you don't love about them, change them! The all time gifted group Earth Wind and Fire sang a song ALL ABOUT LOVE , "You gotta love you, gotta love all the beautiful things around you, the trees and the birds, and if there ain't no beauty you gotta make some beauty." See the moment and then seize the opportunity!! It only takes a second to be too late, so capture what's yours.

I love the Don Miguel Ruiz book, "The Four Agreements," where he shares that 'one should never take a thing personal.' When you take not securing a job or position personally, you are setting yourself up for failure. For all the time you fret and complain about how the job should have been yours is as much time as you could have put into preparing for your next opportunity. My attempts at sulking because of a job not garnered were extremely short-lived. God wouldn't allow me to grovel about a past event; it's gone, now let go, move on, and create the next moment.

The truth just is. When we can somehow remove ourselves from the ordeal at hand, we can see and accept that what we are encountering is just an experience. When we can focus on the here and now, giving our lives, our loves and our passions the best of who we are, is when we really win the best roles, jobs, and opportunities. It never makes sense to fight the flow of truth because it just is. Not embracing or accepting the truth will result in you going down fighting, scratching, kicking, and holding on to a position that doesn't exist. Lots of time, energy and effort are wasted and in the end, the truth will rear its head once again to rule. The saying Truth Rules isn't just a term to be taken lightly. Over any and everything, truth prevails and the closer we get to that understanding the truth, the more free we will feel and more importantly, the more free we will actually BE.

LYTE IS PERSISTENT

Let your light shine where ever you are.

When I was younger, I stayed on the road, touring all over the globe. There were radio tours that required me to fly into a city, wake up at 5am, and head to the radio station. After the station visit, we'd head to a one stop or record store to promote the record. I became accustomed to being away from home on every holiday as well as my birthday.

I worked my butt off month after month performing for sold out crowds with several other acts. You can imagine that once I was able to have any breaks and take time to rest, I did. I slept long and hard for days on end. I loved being off and not having a schedule.

There is no 'getting over' or doing as little as possible just to get a pass. Forget what you've read in those "get success quick" books, there are no shortcuts and the moment you think you can set all your hopes and dreams on a short cut, you may as well say you forfeit. In this life it's about giving the best of what you have in order to reap the best type of benefits. I happen to enjoy options and my experience has been that the best options come only to those who work smart, hard or both.

The wonderful thing about this journey called life is that we all have one of our own. It's our own personal walk that makes us uniquely different from every other person on this planet. When allowing our lives to be led by truth, we all know when there is improvement needed. We know when we've been out of line or some describe it as going off the path. We know when our integrity has been compromised and when we've chosen to act outside of the rules we once saw so fit to set in place for ourselves.

I recall one spring when there was a bit of time to kill and we all decided to go downtown to play handball. Handball happens to be one of my favorite past times that I learned to play in junior high school. I was pretty good too, earning street trophies and taking names as I "Kilt" the ball. Kilt meant I simply slapped the ball with the palm of my hand, hitting it at the right angle causing it to slam precisely between the wall and the ground, leaving it no room to bounce to my opponent.

Well one afternoon my security and I left the office and headed downtown to the handball courts. We arrived around 2:30pm and because the courts were empty, we were able to start right away. We slugged that little blue ball back and forth between the two of us until our hands were blistering red. Hours had gone by and I had not a care in the world for anything else.

Unfortunately, while I was playing handball, I missed an extremely important meeting with the Nike design team who had traveled in from Portland, Oregon. They were in New York wanting to meet with me to design an MC Lyte shoe and I had gone completely missing. I had purposely avoided attending that meeting because I had chosen to go into a "woe is me" stage. In my mind, because I had always worked hard, I felt justified in trying to convince the people around me to support me when I chose to do something against the master plan. What an absolute tragedy and I regret it even to this day that I would be so careless to let a once in a lifetime opportunity pass me by. I was drastically irresponsible and I have paid for it ever since.

Had I stopped for one moment and really examined the benefits of the meeting and the repercussions of not going, I may have been able to make a wiser decision. If I'd had someone around me who even understood, perhaps they would have said something to influence and help me with making a better choice. Today I understand what it means to have someone in my corner who gets my mission and can hold me accountable for doing, on a consistent basis, the things that are necessary for me to get what it is I say I want.

In some ways, I was never able to recover from that deal. I've done lots of things with Nike and several other brands, but nothing would have been greater than having an MC Lyte shoe to commemorate a moment in history for Brooklyn, NY, Female MCs, etc. Of course, that ordeal skyrocketed my comprehension of taking advantage of opportunities when they arrive. It helped me to get serious about my life and my business. All the day-to-day work that had been done over the years had created a moment like that and I failed to realize it at the time. Honestly speaking, I was a brat and wanted my way for the moment and because of it I lost out on bringing a vision to fruition, one that I had dreamt of for many years prior to that time.

Living in the light primarily means living with truth -- your truth -- the belief that you hold on to and has made your foundation what it is. I claim responsibility for having lost the potential of that deal and not handling my choices properly. Being persistently in the light means prioritizing and staying focused on the goals you've set forth for yourself. It means knowing and acknowledging that long before the moment of deviation, there was a plan; and not doing what the plan dictates means that I have moved away from the light. The light provides the truth and when guided down a path of righteousness there is no way the light can fail you.

LYTE EQUALS FREEDOM

The truth shall make you free.

Living in the light means having the ability to be who you are, cover to cover, from the inside out, without any connection to the effects of potential judgment from others. This freedom in being yourself is the key to any and all healthy relationships.

I believe what plagued my relationships most was my inability to just let go and be seen. For so many years, I masked my feelings and thoughts behind wanting to be seen in the "politically correct" light. I remember dating one gentleman and having deep considerations about whether I should spend more time with him; especially since I wasn't sure that I wanted to be in a relationship with him. What would be the message if I called him too many times? And really, what qualifies as too many times? How silly was it for me to put a limit to how many times I could speak to him and a limit to how long I should speak at any given moment. I was conflicted: I didn't want to lead him on, although I did enjoy spending time with him, but I wanted to appear cool, calm and collected so he wouldn't think I liked him too much. Truthfully, I was into him as much as he was into me . . . maybe even more. So what was I doing? Playing it safe? Guarding my heart? Whatever I was doing was a mystery even to me . . . and what I do know now is that it didn't feel like freedom; it wasn't the truth.

Saving face all those years has kept me good and single. I kept pretending until finally I decided that the truth was a prerequisite for receiving all that I wanted in life. I had to get real with everything in order to see the trees while I was in the forest.

In my relationships, I had learned to give enough just to get by. I never became too attached because I wanted to easily let go whenever I felt I was ready. This was a protective mechanism I had learned earlier in life that supposedly helped in preserving my feelings at the cost of another's. A lack of trust in others put me in a space where I was a afraid to get too close to anyone.

In my twenties I went through feelings of insecurity and low self esteem when it came to relationships. I was confident and certain when it came to business, however it was a completely different story when it came to love. "Was I good enough?" "Why would he stay and my daddy didn't?" Sounds pretty simple and of no significance to some, but there are many who understand these troubles. That's when I began to run away from any and all opportunities to build meaningful relationships based on truth and commitment. My silly notion was this: if I stood still in honesty and committed to the process of falling in love, I'd be trampled, used, and thrown away. I walked with a deep mistrust of men and lumped them all in one category, which I later learned was something I had fabricated from nothing that was real.

While living in fear and running from the truth, I ultimately participated in relationships I didn't have to commit to. I was too frightened to become emotionally involved with anyone so I skirted about relationships without ever entering completely. If there wasn't a way out, I created it. I've encountered times in my life where everything was hidden -- my behavior and my feelings. I frequently took the stand that if people wanted to change, they would do so on their own and that meant I wouldn't have to tell them what I didn't like or appreciate. I believed that people were going to be who they were and who was I to tell anyone about something I didn't like about "them."

Because I never communicated what I wanted that was different than what I was seeing or receiving, things would eventually get to a boiling point and then I'd conveniently leave. Honestly, I had secretly created a way out by letting things surmount to a point that would justify me walking away without turning back. I let a fatherless childhood push me into a fearful place when it came to opening up and submitting to the journey of building a successful relationship. I do not even recall how many times I've landed myself in a relationship where it inevitably ended in a less than favorable manor -- times when I acted irrationally and made decisions that would later come back to haunt me. I do not regret any experiences I've had with past relationships. They served a purpose in helping me to grow and understand the concept of union and what it actually takes to create a lasting one.

Finally, after all these years, I began to understand that listening to my intuition can and will always play a key factor in making life altering decisions. I have entered into relationships that weren't a proper fit from the beginning and that's a huge problem for quite a few of us. We meet someone, they're interesting, we become excited about learning all of who they are. We become enthralled with talking about our lives and history into the late night hours. We see and notice aspects of them that may not be aligned with our own personality much less what we truly want. Many times I chose to overlook those things and they later became catastrophic differences. It was like attempting to put a square peg into a round hole. No matter how gently you maneuver that square peg, it will never fit into that round hole.

I've learned the hard way what happens when I am disobedient to the rules I've set for myself. In pursuing relationships that aren't seeded in light, truth and freedom, a good line of questioning might be:

1. Does this person match my level of integrity?
2. Is this person completely free to engage in a relationship?
3. Can I be proud of this union?

There was a point in time and space when I decided to get out of my own way and allow God to lead. I begin to make every effort to live free. That meant relinquishing all preconceived beliefs about who I SHOULD be and embracing the truth about who I actually am. I finally had to take a step back and view the entire picture. I had to discover what I really needed to have the level of ultimate happiness I wanted. I needed to receive every individual for who they were. Just as I expected others to accept me with all my flaws and imperfections.

I began to make every effort to live openly and in the light. That meant relinquishing all imaginative ideas about what life should look like and embrace more of what life *IS*. I was no longer concerned with what it looked like to other people but became more in-tuned with what felt good to me. I had spent a life of taking the easy way out, but more importantly, I had spent a life of choosing to not live in the light and remaining in that space was no longer going to work for me in any way.

I was no longer going to minimize my desire for a healthy, loving relationship because of my fears to really get in one and make it happen. I now wake every morning wanting to be seen and I am in an adamant search to find those who can take, withstand and understand my truth. Sometimes all that is needed is a trusting situation between family, lovers and/or friends to then feel the comfort in being seen completely for who you are. To stand by what you believe and what you feel passionately about takes courage. At times we'll be forced to take a stand even when we are not assured of understanding on the other end. We can never be certain when someone will or won't understand our position on any given subject and whether we choose to express it is completely up to us as individuals.

I can honestly say I don't regret a day of love. That means I don't look back on being in love and say I wish that wouldn't have happened. It was all for a reason and each relationship presented different experiences that have helped me grow and get closer to the person I'm pushing to become. I have learned to appreciate that every circumstance that I may have viewed as painful or intolerable actually pushed me further along on my path to truth and freedom.

FOCUS ON THE LYTE

*Give your attention to what you want;
ignore everything else.*

Due to the high level of interaction and information available in this world, there are multitudes of distractions that can lead you down a path not fit for anyone to travel. It's grueling and life itself can feel like it's betrayed us all. Trying to maintain stamina, let alone confidence, can completely bend a person who is not ready completely out of shape. Remaining focused on what is RIGHT is tricky and complicated. Growing up in New York City, I know what it means to lose focus and to lose your way by literally getting off track.

Throughout my career, I've allowed people and things to serve as a cushion to my ego at a high price. I gave attention to things that weren't of the light, which caused me to spend much of my time in the dark. I speak of the dark as an unknowingness of my power and my purpose. In return for my attention, I received admiration and what I thought was love. I've learned someone in your circle must have the sight of light if you don't. It is, of course, there for all to see and succumb to, however it is always good to be surrounded by people who have an awareness of the light and it's power. I like to think of them as angels that lead you back to the light when you've wandered off the path into the abyss, where many others would love for you to stay.

When the Hip Hop tide had changed and it was time for me to make moves to survive, I tripped into resentment. I felt there weren't enough voices of women reporting on and within our culture.

Female representation was null and void. I resented the change and I detested everything that began to inevitably happen with the genre and the culture of Hip Hop. I groaned and complained about it all to anyone who would listen. I griped over my disgust with the lyrics, images and lack of positivity.

Somewhere in the midst of groveling, I discovered that the negativity that existed in the music was now spilling over into my everyday train of thought. Instead of pointing my influence into a positive direction for seekers of light to follow, I plummeted to the depths of the basement. My wakeup call came when a young producer suggested that I leave the business if I was no longer happy with participating in Hip Hop. I thought to myself 'is he crazy'?!?! That short discussion turned me completely around and I began to understand my power and influence in the business. I decided to walk into the light with all my negative thinking and release it. My lack of leadership wouldn't be tolerated any more. I had to step up front and continue my mission of educating young girls about the importance of defining themselves for themselves. The impression I needed to leave with the next generation of Hip Hop lovers could not be one of defeat, but instead, that of victory. I had to focus on what could be done; not on how unhappy I was about what had already taken place.

I can recall minor setbacks that took my focus away from the intended goals and I realize that as long as I didn't look for the light, I remained lost. When you are hit with adversities the key is to not stop your mission but to continue with a vengeance. Throughout my career I've experienced times when my excitement for an opportunity was met with contention, and at that point, I'd lose energy and put my focus somewhere else. I realize now that not everyone is deserving of my attention. Not all things require my time of day.

Part of focusing on the light is really drilling into what your God given purpose is and not allowing anything to turn you away from it. When you remain tuned into what you are here to do, no one and nothing can hinder your actions. In fact, when it is what God has intended for you, all things will work for the GOOD.

Focus requires time and effort and without having a reservoir of those ingredients, it's impossible to remain aligned with what's important. I tend to think when time is focused on the light, the rest of life falls into place. It is a letting go of trying to see all there is and a relinquishing of attempting to know everything. It is putting your faith and trust in the Supreme Power of God that emanates all the light we will ever need. We need not waste time on trying to figure out how the vision He implanted in us will take form. If we can just stay focused and open to where the light will lead, we will arrive.

Focusing on the light means to stay engaged in this present moment with positivity, with the light representing all that is good, wholesome and true. When bad things happen, we are not meant to wallow in the mire. We are not meant to be thrown so far off the tracks that we can no longer see the light and somehow even forget that its illumination exists.

When you have experienced a seemingly unforgivable act, it is only cruel to one's self to hold on to such an injustice. Keeping our hearts and minds filled with the love of light is the only way to make it fully into a space of truth. Always keeping our consciousness in the moment we reside in will result in true happiness. Do nothing with the heartache of yesterday or the worry of tomorrow, but release and let it all go and stay focused on the light of today.

LOVE EQUALS LYTE

Love is the strongest and most powerful energy source.

Lord knows I have looked for love in all the wrong places and had to either be jolted into reality or moved slowly into TRUTH. In either case, when you refuse to submit to darkness you will sometimes experience rude awakenings. For a spirit of light to remain in the darkness it requires unconsciousness, however when God calls you from your slumber.... you MUST move. The light He shines to awaken your spirit is the pure love needed to make you whole. I have firmly proclaimed publicly, I love who loves me. I, in this day, still accentuate this point, however I now know what LOVE truly is.

Long ago I thought attention equaled love. I believed that if someone decided to pay me some attention for a long enough period of time and they actually said the three words, that it must be true. I later found out that many who profess to love someone haven't a clue what LOVE truly is. They are doing and giving the best that they can, yet love is not for those who choose to reside in the darkness. Love is not ownership nor is it lust. Love is truth and if lived in the light, it forever remains.

I am now open to receive love in all forms because the love I give is pure without contingencies. Because I can give of an honest love, I can have an honest love that is meant to do me well and not harm or strip away who I am: love that is meant to help me grow and does not impede upon my life in the light and as long as I am living in the light, I can see what LOVE is and what it is not.

In this business I've been blessed to be a part of, I am respectfully admired and adored by many and I do not take that for granted. With the level of openness and commitment to remain a vessel of light for God to use and for all to see, much is required of me. I take on this responsibility with everything I am and I do not shun it; rather I embrace it. I simply love connecting with people through the inspiration I am able to impart. Seeing my brothers and sisters smile who are otherwise struggling to keep their spirits on high means the world to me. If for just a short time I am able to uplift someone's character or the morale of a community, I am doing the job I was sent to do. I am living in light and in my purpose and that alone allows for LOVE to be experienced throughout my work.

When you can successfully love all mankind, including every race, gender, creed and religion, then you can attest to living in the light. In the heart of every man, woman and child resides the love of GOD, therefore making the light attainable for all. Living in the light is not as difficult as one might think. Many see the light that exists in others and feel it is not theirs to have, when in fact the supply is infinite. Admiring the light that emanates from others is just a testament that what you've seen can be and is your reflection.

The same quality that you witness in others that you long to possess already dwells within you. The same concept applies to the qualities you find in others that are less than stellar, they too are recognized because they exist within you as well. Your job is simply to find your way and to know that the gut feeling about who you are and what you see -- truth or lie, good or bad, beautiful or ugly -- is just that. Don't try to turn what you see into something else. Embrace what it is and if it needs to be changed, do so with love and kindness and before you try to change others, change yourself.

Like attracts like and for every moment you make contact with another human being, you are experiencing you. You, from second to second, are being met with you. If you are met with contention, living in the light would lead you to alter what it is that you're giving out to attract that contention.

Once while I was in the midst of a discussion with a friend, I felt him being a bit ornery and immediately I had to check myself. Now of course every time someone else is behaving distastefully doesn't mean I am, but it certainly throws up a flag for me to remain myself in the exchange. It's so simple and easy to react identical to what it is you perceive you are receiving. More times than not, we can get swept away with how we're being spoken to and even though we're not fond of it, we'll give it right back. To reach for the light in every encounter is the key to experiencing the fullness of love; never stop aiming for the understanding of what it means to have it, own it and use it.

I don't know anyone who is perfect or displays perfect behavior in every scenario, but if we can just try to be good to others, the light guarantees that the goodness will be reciprocated somehow, some way. Try to overlook negativity and allow light to consume your heart and mind so that you may move peacefully through this journey of life.

FREE THOUGHT, FREE ENERGY and FREEDOM TO LOVE are what keeps a person's spirit on high. The room to think freely and have ideas heard keep the energy of love, light and freedom moving and not stagnant. And love....well you know love, it's that one single element that makes life possible to be endured. It is the reason above all reasons. Love is why one will sacrifice their thoughts, time and energy towards living in the light.

LYTE SHINES BEST IN THE DARKNESS

Darkness in the light is just a shadow, and that shadow must follow you, you don't follow it. So shine!

There comes a time in your life when you really get down to the wire. Your back is up against the wall. It's just you and God. A time when you face the music about who you are, who you are not, what could have, should have and would have been . . . that moment when you stand before Him and in all of your imperfection, you give it to Him so you can be made whole. It's a letting go, a confession of sorts, and question and answer session, and or it might be as simple as asking for forgiveness. Whatever it is, you know it's that time when you make a major breakthrough and cross into another level of real living. Living in the light.

I've experienced that. Along this path of living in the Lyte, there were times when I knew that what I was choosing wasn't completely right for me or others. In my search to better myself, I realize in those times I may have let others down, but more importantly, I let myself down. But when I simply expressed all of it to God, I felt a new power and renewed energy . . . I felt the power of God's love embracing all of me and my imperfections while molding me to be who it is that I desired to become.

My belief in a better day has pulled me through the most arduous of tasks and the most difficult work: inner work that one can only do for oneself. There is no prescription that can help anyone aide in addressing all that must be altered in one's life. There may be angels who stop along your path, but not until YOU are truly ready to submit and go the way of the light will change occur.

For me, I had always been on a quest for the knowledge of life. I longed to know about the moon, sun and stars, but it wasn't until I began the quest of understanding how my actions affected others, did I truly learn my power: a power that only God could have blessed me with. I also learned that when used carelessly or unknowingly, that same power can bring about pain and unhappiness.

In my younger years, I spent much of my time hiding from feelings. In my attempt to not ever experience the hurt of a broken heart brought on by relationships or friendships, I kept everyone and everything at bay. I witnessed the unhappiness of my mother and relationships gone sour. I saw firsthand the pain and how debilitating a break up can be. I wished for nothing less than a life of never having to feel pain. Unknowingly, as I wished away the feeling of pain, so went the feeling of true happiness and anything else that ultimately had the ability to tap into my heart. I looked out at all the love surrounding me and wanted the depth of a real relationship, however at that time, I was unprepared to give what it took.

You know, when you see the couple that's been together for 40 years or the successful children reared to succeed or the tennis player who goes straight to the top, it all took work. In most cases, it took work that called for a relentless attitude and an ambition to keep moving when everything else was set against the goal. In order to move to the next level, I had to prepare myself to work on ME.

I needed to take better care of myself to even know what I could truly give to another. The self work had to take priority over anything else: the kind of investigation and inspecting that one isn't accustomed to administering to one's self. I had to be willing to turn over rocks to get to myself and be willing to see things that were less than pretty: the shadows that remain hidden until one is completely ready to face truth with light. Prior to this awareness, my family, friends and lovers merely received the pieces I was willing to surrender. I gave just enough to keep control and with this tactic, I never had to 'feel' a thing. Emotions were for the weak and I never wanted to get trapped in my feelings, as I believed it would give others the power to take me down. Unfortunately, it was all about me and in order to safeguard my heart, I didn't allow anyone close enough to cause havoc or inevitably bring love.

All while protecting myself from being hurt, I ended up hurting others. I remained closed off to communication, I ended the possibilities of long lasting love, and with that behavior, I pushed many positive and loving people away.

When I recall less than favorable decisions I've made, they may not have resulted in the desired outcome, but they've certainly taught me valuable lessons: the types of lessons no one could impart audibly, but rather, lessons that one has to come face to face with because no one else's story could give them a better perspective. They must be learned empirically. The lessons I have learned about power have left such an impression that I now want my entire life guided by the source of power that keeps all: God and His infinite light.

In my darkest hours, I've found that nothing appears more clear than the light of God. That light shows in many ways, but it's the brightest for those who are seeking the way. I have learned to depend on the light to lead me out of a darkness I thought it was impossible to leave.

No matter the darkness, be it confusion, career stagnation, abuse, alcohol, drugs, or any and all addictions, the light exists for all to see and have. If only a ray is what you see, follow it and remain steadfast until you are fully immersed. The one thing I know for sure is that there is always a way out of darkness, and it's never too late to get out. The key? Never give up the search for what is right and just. Your heart knows what's right, so if your goal is to live your purpose, the light will guide your path if you let go and believe. Your winning is dependent upon your faith.

Throughout time I've heard "Let GO, Let God" so often that if I had a dollar for each time I heard it, well you know the rest. It's taken some time for me to understand and practice this concept. Being an A personality and a determined individual, it was pretty challenging for me to let go of anything. And although I understand the words and what they mean, it still takes discipline to not involve myself with things that GOD will handle. I can't tell you how many times I've walked myself into the darkness and looked up to find I've lost sight of my purpose. But If I would just wait on the light to arrive, then I'd be able to see all that's before me. I am at my best when I allow the light to lead.

Amongst the muck and mud, light is still to be seen. Love still rules and GOD is ALL. I am forever in a state of gratitude that God is an all forgiving God and that

He will shine His light for all eternity. When all seems as though it has fallen to pieces, His light continues to shine for all to find and His only hope is that you will trust Him and walk in it.

Join the Movement:
www.hiphopsistersnetwork.org

About Hip-Hop Sisters Network
Founded by MC Lyte, the legendary lyricist and iconic hip-hop pioneer, Hip Hop Sisters Network is a non-profit organization that promotes positive images of women of ethnic diversity, bringing leaders from the world of Hip Hop, the entertainment industry, and the corporate world.

HHSN provides national and international support to women and youth around the globe on the topics of:

Cultural Issues;

Financial Empowerment;

Health and Wellness;

Mentorship; and

Educational Opportunities.

Celebrity advisory board members include Faith Evans, Ledisi, Jada Pinkett Smith, Chilli, Russell Simmons, Cheryl "Salt" James, Malinda Williams, Kelly Price, Malcolm Jamal Warner, and Dr. Benjamin Chavis.

Hip Hop Sisters Network welcomes and embraces partnership opportunities with individuals and institutions that contribute to the empowerment of people across the globe.

About MC Lyte

Lyricist, pioneer, icon, inspirational speaker, veteran, philanthropist, and entrepreneur describe one of the most prolific and well-respected female Hip Hop artists of our time: **Lana "MC Lyte" Moorer**. A pioneer in the industry, she opened the door for future female Hip Hop artists by daring to do what had never been done while doing something she loved. A role model to women and respected by men everywhere, Lyte never compromises who she is and consistently displays that a woman can turn heads fully clothed! Whenever possible, **Lyte,** as she is affectionately known by her inner circle, enjoys traveling across the nation to use her expertise and story of success to motivate others to take ownership of the world around them while striving to be the best they can possibly be.

Author of "**Unstoppable: Igniting the Power Within to Achieve Your Greatest Potential**," **MC Lyte** is also very active in many social projects, including anti-violence campaigns and Rock the Vote.

MC Lyte is the Founder/Chairman of Hip Hop Sisters Foundation, Inc. the President/CEO of Sunni Gyrl, Inc., a global entertainment firm, the immediate past President of the Los Angeles Chapter of the Recording Academy (Grammy Organization) and she is also a proud honorary member of Sigma Gamma Rho Sorority, Inc.